REPORT WRITING

Guidelines for Information Workers

Pat F. Booth

REPORT WRITING

Guidelines for information workers
Pat F Booth

BASIC BOOKS FOR INFORMATION WORKERS SERIES

No. 1

Basic Bibliography Book

Rosslyn Nicholas & Albert E Standley

The first of a series of booklets designed to provide basic, practical guidance to information workers (and students). Of use to anyone who 'wishes to produce and present a list of documents and/or other information-containing material which will be comprehensive for and comprehensible to those for whom it is intended'. Indexed.

A5 pbk £2.95 isbn 0 946139 15 6

Published 1.1984

REPORT WRITING

Guidelines for Information Workers

Pat F. Booth

© Pat F Booth, 1985

Published by Elm Publications, Seaton House,
Kings Ripton, Cambs PE17 2NJ and printed and
bound by Mossprint, Alresford, Colchester.

No part of this book may be reproduced or transmitted
in any form or by any means without prior, written
permission from the publisher.
January, 1985.

 British Library Cataloguing in Publication Data

```
Booth, Pat F.
   Report writing.
   1. Report writing
   I. Title
   808'.06602021      PE1478

   ISBN 0-946139-30-X
```

BSDCS7

CONTENTS

Introduction	vii
1. The report – a form of written communication	1
2. Purpose, topic and message (why, what and for whom)	5
3. Structure and content	8
4. Style, language and tone	23
5. Copy preparation and reproduction	28
6. Reports for particular purposes	34
7. Launching the report – and afterwards	43
References	46
Further reading	49
Index	50

FORTHCOMING IN 1985

Basic Reference & Information Work

Peter Jackaman

Sewn pbk   isbn 0 946139 11 3

INTRODUCTION

Several excellent books dealing with report writing already exist; it seems necessary, therefore, to explain the appearance of another publication on the same subject.

The majority of works so far published are concerned either with writing in general or with the requirements for report writing in contexts such as science, engineering, management, business and research – the latter group presenting information related to those contexts, with allied examples and vocabulary. This is not to imply that these publications are irrelevant to the needs of information workers – indeed there is much in them that can be read with profit, and reference to them is recommended throughout this text.

Information workers (librarians, information scientists, archivists, indexers, bibliographers, database managers, information officers – and all the other titles by which such workers may be known), as well as those training to be information workers, are required to produce reports for many different purposes and within a variety of subject environments. This publication sets out only to suggest guidelines for the production of reports in those information-oriented environments; in most cases the principles are the same – no matter what the context – but a particular situation may demand a certain emphasis, selected set of actions or specific content features.

These guidelines cannot guarantee perfection or success – since, as there is always room for personal predilection, there is no single standard for a perfect or successful report. It is hoped that, at least, report writers (particularly those about to make their first attempt) will be assisted in overcoming their uncertainties and in organising their thoughts, expressing them in the most appropriate manner and format, and having them take effect in the fulfilment of their intentions.

Few publications are entirely original in their content; I acknowledge with thanks the friends, colleagues, students and course participants with whom discussions about communication, writing, reports and copy preparation have provided ideas and examples, and the previous writers in those fields whose works have given me interest and pleasure.

PFB
August 1984

ABOUT THE AUTHOR

Pat Booth, MEd BA ALA ACP MIInfSci, is an information specialist and lecturer who has practised information work in industrial, research and government environments and has taught information retrieval studies at Ealing College of Higher Education, London.

ABOUT THE BOOK

'Report writing: guidelines for information workers' is intended to assist those working in information environments and those who are studying to do so, who are required to write reports on such topics as student projects, research, professional or personal development, financial matters, system evaluations, accommodation, departmental activities, meetings and personnel.

It sets out background and suggestions within a perspective which looks first at the report as a form of written communication, then at the identification of purpose, topic and message; structure and content are examined, together with the selection of appropriate style, language and tone. Methods and problems of copy preparation and reproduction are reviewed and the special characteristics of reports for particular purposes highlighted; the concluding chapter deals with the launching of the finished report.

A substantial list of references and further reading is included and there is an index to the complete text.

CHAPTER 1 : THE REPORT — A FORM OF WRITTEN COMMUNICATION

DEFINITION

An appropriate definition of a **report** (within the context of this publication) has to be considered first in relation to the concept of **communication**, which is to do with the imparting of **information**, and then more specifically as a kind of **written record** within which imparted information is contained, stored and utilised.

Dictionary definitions of 'report' include a range of meanings, but those most useful to our present needs refer to a statement of a formal nature, containing facts or a record of some kind, and resulting from an investigation or study. The emphasis is clearly on the need for some intellectual and methodical processing of sought-out data which have been gathered for the purpose of drawing conclusions, making recommendations, surveying the scene, or conveying to others information about the state of something, whether an organisation, a system, a procedure, a person or a piece of equipment. The report is not, from these definitions, to be seen as an impulsive and impassioned outburst with no prior checking of data or assembly of evidence.

On the other hand, there may be occasions when another common definition may be felt apposite: the explosive noise also called a 'report' may be suggestive of a document* intended to create a disturbance, provoke agitated discussion or hasten action.

There are several other terms in common use which also refer to formal or official 'factual' documents and whose meanings overlap with those given to 'report'. They include: memorandum, statement, account, minutes, record, paper, bulletin, briefing document, communiqué, working paper, discussion paper, case history, profile and dossier; all may be used at some time to denote what has been referred to above as a report. They are not all entirely equivalent in meaning; particular situations give rise to their own terminology and nuances — 'minutes' being associated with the proceedings of a meeting, and 'bulletins' being assumed to consist of new, updating information. Sometimes these terms carry

---
* The term 'document' is used throughout this text to refer to a written record of any kind.

implications about internal structure or the form in which the finished document is expected to appear: a 'briefing document' presents factual information in a structured form which can be quickly assimilated, and a 'memorandum' is usually short and written in the language and style used between members of the same organisation. It is important, therefore, when a request to produce a document is received, to ascertain precisely which particular end-product is required; this may save the writer the frustration and embarrassment of supplying an inappropriate type for the purpose.

What emerges from this discussion is that reports (whatever term is used) are documents usually written to fulfil clearly identified and immediate formal or official functions and are constrained by those functions; writers may themselves formulate the functions, or have them imposed upon them by others. Reports are not normally works of the free, unfettered, creative imagination, using a full range of imagery, inventive vocabulary and eccentric, elaborate or peculiar style. However, this should not mean that they are flat, uninteresting collections of undistinguished prose — care should be taken to use language, style and tone in an engaging way, so that the readers (perhaps despite themselves) will be quickly interested.

Information workers, and intending information workers, may become involved in a variety of situations demanding the writing of different kinds of reports. Specific attention is given to some of these in Chapter 6, but a typical list might include reports on: a student project; the progress and outcome of a meeting; a technical equipment evaluation; staff development; departmental activities; professional progress; financial requirements; attendance at a conference; the business and activities of a society, club or other association; a management problem; a study visit.

ORAL AND WRITTEN COMMUNICATION

We impart and exchange information in several ways; the oral (spoken) and the written (using letters and numerals imposed on a surface) methods are two of the most common, and it is pertinent to review the specific advantages of each.

Oral communication has an immediacy and a personal touch which can be difficult to catch in the written method. This arises partly from the physical senses (vision, hearing, touch) which can be utilised by speakers and listeners and partly from the range of tones, volumes, expressions and speeds within which speech can be presented in order to achieve attention, emphasise a point, create a diversion and so on. In addition, there is often (not always) an informality and a flexibility which permit an interchange (of query and answer, comment and response) between the sender and the receiver of the 'message'.

Written communication lacks these qualities but possesses others – not available in the oral method – which enhance it and, in many cases, make it more effective. Whereas speech tends to be informal, writing – perhaps because it is more considered and presented 'at a distance' – gives a more formal perspective and thus can suggest greater authority and trustworthiness. Written documents have the possibility of becoming permanent records (which unrecorded speech does not), of being read again and again, quoted from, their details checked, perused at the individual reader's own best reading speed, commented on by a large readership (perhaps critically); the data included and the statements made are therefore more likely to be ascertained as valid and accurate, and the life of the message extended through continuing use.

When writing, therefore, it is relevant to bear in mind the advantages of the written method and to exploit them to the full; it is also necessary to be aware of what may be lost by not being able to address the recipient face to face, and to try to compensate by introducing an element of immediacy and personal involvement through the style, vocabulary level and tone employed.

REPORT WRITING – DECISIONS

The writing of a report involves decisions concerning

a) the **purpose** for which it is being written
b) the specific **topic**
c) the precise **message** to be delivered
d) the appropriate **structure** (reports are expected to have a recognisable shape and development, rather than to 'ramble')

e) suitable **length** and **format**,
f) the right **vocabulary**, **style** and **tone**,
g) the amount and kind of supporting **evidence** or **data**.

The writer's responsibility may (and should) also extend at least to consideration, if not execution, of the **design**, physical **presentation** and **production** of the finished document, its **distribution** and (depending on circumstances) **follow-up** after copies have been circulated.

The remaining chapters are devoted to further discussion of these matters.

CHAPTER 2 : PURPOSE, TOPIC AND MESSAGE (WHY, WHAT AND FOR WHOM)

PURPOSE

Before starting to write, it is essential to establish the reason why the report is to be produced – this helps in making decisions on length, tone, language, physical format and other aspects.

Not all reports are written voluntarily, let alone with enthusiasm; the need to produce a document may be regarded as a chore which has to be undertaken on a regular basis so as to keep others (colleagues, members) informed, or as a 'once and for all' obstacle to be overcome in order to gain a qualification or aid promotion, or as a means of encouraging (or preventing) further investigation, among a variety of perceptions. Some reports may arise undemanded from a strong emotion felt by someone who has something to say but who has no regular channel for its expression – perhaps in connection with an idea for a new development, or frustration over inadequate performance of a system; in these cases, just as much as the others, care is needed in clarifying the purpose, pinpointing the topic and message and selecting the style.

TOPIC AND MESSAGE

The writer will find it useful to note down the topic (subject) of the report at the outset; this may be done in general terms and may, finally, be reflected in the title. Some writers find it remarkably easy to stray from the main subject without realising it, and to have it stated and kept before them while writing can help them stick to the point; a report on a junior colleague's professional development should not digress into the working experiences and management problems of the writer, for example, and one on departmental activities during the past year should not give a detailed account of events which took place three years before.

It is not essential at this stage to decide on the final title which the completed report will carry. The choice may, in fact, be limited by custom – in the case of a departmental progress report, a running title is probably already established, requiring only differentiation by date. If a free choice of title is permitted, it is best to select one which is indicative of the subject, concise and easy to memorise; humorous titles are not recommended as they can be ambiguous when standing on their own, as titles often do in catalogues and bibliographies. Additional information can be added as a subtitle — though this may not be included when the title appears in records compiled by others.

Most significantly, the precise message to be transmitted in the report must be identified; that is, the specific package of information which the writer wishes the readers to receive and understand. This 'kernel' must be what comes out clearly when the document is ready — supported, explained and justified, but not obscured, by the remainder of the text, and enclothed in the 'right' style, language and physical format. There must be no doubt in the readers' minds as to the overall conclusion or proposal put forward.

The message does not always have to be stated explicitly, in direct terms — indeed, it is sometimes better if it is not, leading the readers to the appropriate conclusions by means of thoughtful and discreet suggestion. A report intended to show that the writer is a highly efficient and effective manager/assistant/supervisor/analyst or reference librarian, popular with colleagues and worthy of promotion to a higher grade, should probably not say so in those words, but should indicate it by describing the individual's progress, achievements and plans. On the other hand, the writer of a report who has to record personal failure and responsibility for a catastrophe may make a better impression by being completely honest and directly admitting it, while at the same time indicating that the reasons are understood, that lessons have been learned, that an unexpectedly beneficial spin-off has occurred or that plans have already been put in train for a remedy or a revised system.

While the report is being composed, the message must be borne in mind and never forgotten; when complete, the whole document must be read through to ensure that the message does stand out and is obvious to the reader. If attempting to provoke action, the report should indicate the need for action and the nature of the action to be taken; the writer wishing to conceal something should endeavour to transmit a message to the effect that all is well and that no further investigation is needed.

Having identified the message, the writer should choose the best position (or positions) in the report for it to be stated clearly. A report should have a structure which frames the message and provides appropriate places for it. Frequently, if the report is long, there is a need for the message to be restated (see Repetition on page 26); inclusion in a summary or abstract is useful also for those recipients who are not likely to have the time or interest (or are too lazy) to peruse the complete document.

RECIPIENTS (POTENTIAL READERS)

Since most writers hope that their works will be read, it is worth considering who will be the recipients of the finished report. They should be viewed both as a group and as individuals — recognition of their characteristics will assist in the choice of appropriate content, structure, format, style and language (as well as determining the number of copies to be reproduced). As a group, they may be colleagues, officials of an organisation, members of an association, tutors, junior staff, government department representatives, interested lay people or the public at large. As individuals, they may be familiar with the subject and its unique vocabulary, totally ignorant of it, 'well-educated', unused to dealing with detailed documents, non-fluent readers of English — a wide range of characteristics can exist within the potential readership.

The finished document should be one which the recipients will wish to read and will understand (unless part of the purpose is to 'blind them with science').

DISTRIBUTION

The extent of distribution must also be ascertained; certain reports will be available to anyone who wishes copies, while others will be graded 'classified' or 'confidential'; some will be free of charge, others priced and commercially published. Some recipients may be sent only the summary, others the full report. The anticipated pattern of distribution will also affect the way in which the report is written, in particular with regard to specific content and the general tone.

CHAPTER 3 : STRUCTURE AND CONTENT

Once the specific message to be transmitted has been identified, the next steps are to decide on the best way of presenting it and to select the most appropriate supporting material. For example — depending upon the nature of the message and the existing state of knowledge of the intended recipients — it may be necessary first to set out a background of information so that readers will understand what follows, or to create an atmosphere of success by describing progress made, before dealing with a less fortunate event; statistical data may be needed to support claims made, or illustrations to clarify plans or system operations.

STRUCTURE

The aim should be to make the finished document flow by

a) starting with a section which sets the scene and engages the interest of the reader

b) gradually introducing — in a logical sequence — other material to inform, explain and justify

c) finishing with a summarising, reminding or rounding-off section — which may contain a statement of recommendations or conclusions.

Even a single-page report should have clearly identifiable introduction, development and conclusion sections. With longer reports it is even more important that an internal structure should be established and adhered to, to ensure comprehensive treatment of the subject, suitable delivery of the message, and speedy retrieval and checking. It is often necessary for readers to be able to pick out particular sections for a second look as a reminder of certain facts or data; structuring aids this, in conjunction with the contents list and the index.

The exact structure and sequence of sections is determined, in each case, by the characteristics and circumstances pertaining to the individual report. Some typical arrangements of major sections are:

a) Summary
   Background
   Scope of the study
   Method
   Conclusions
   Glossary
   Bibliography

b) Introduction
   The present situation
   Options for change
   Recommendations
   References

b) Abstract
   Context
   Objectives
   Issues raised
   Proposals
   Appendixes

d) Preface
   System requirements
   Systems available
   Criteria for selection
   The final choice
   Appendix: System data sheets

The structures above do not cover all requirements, but are intended to show broadly how text can be divided into meaningful sections. Each of the sections named may be divided and given subheadings, and those subsections may in turn be further divided — as much as is necessary for clarity.

The structure is often entirely within the control of the writer, but sometimes it is dictated by convention or custom — periodic progress reports may always have to follow the same pattern, in order to facilitate comparison of data between one period and another, for example, and visit and personnel reports may have their structure specified by standard forms which have to be completed. Before starting, writers must acquaint themselves with any previous reports which exist and with the individual requirements laid down by the organisations requesting or sponsoring the reports.

Emphasising the structure

Structuring is assisted by headings, subheadings, section or paragraph numbering, indentation and variations in size and style of lettering. Headings such as those suggested above may be given numbers (or letters), with any subsection headings numbered decimally so as to show subordination of subsection to section.

For example:

1	INTRODUCTION	or A	
	1.1 Background	A1	
	1.2 Scope of the study	A2	
2	METHODOLOGY	B	
	2.1 Interviews	B1	
	2.1.1 Staff		B1.1
	2.1.2 Public		B1.2
	2.2 Observations	B2	
3	FINDINGS	C	
4	RECOMMENDATIONS	D	
	4.1 Short-term	D1	
	4.2 Long-term	D2	

For some reports, it is felt necessary to number every paragraph and subparagraph, so that each one can be uniquely identified and referred to, but in most cases the numbering of sections alone, or of sections and subsections, is adequate. Whichever system is employed, it should be remembered that its aim is to assist clarification and quick identification of specific parts of the report, and to aid cross-referencing from one part to another; it may also help in the preparation of the index, where section or paragraph numbers can be used instead of, or as well as, page numbers (see page 20).

CONTENT

The main text

The content of the main body of the text should be restricted to what is necessary for the message to be effectively expressed and transmitted; the information presented should be relevant and concise, reflect a logical development from one stage to the next and be provided with the right amount of explanation for the anticipated readership. A chronology of events may be useful but should not dominate the content. Anecdotes, irrelevant accounts of personal experiences and unsubstantiated opinions should be excluded. Detailed analyses, compilations of data and illustrations which are not essential for immediate comprehension of the points made may be better placed in appendixes, rather than in the main text, but care must be taken to indicate in the text that they exist and where they may be found. Advice on the gathering of data may be found in Moore (1983). Items such as title page information, lists of illustrations, foreword or preface, summary or abstract, contents list, lists of bibliographical references, further reading and glossaries must be appropriately placed before and after the main text.

Footnotes

On occasion it may be suitable to provide explanatory or background information in the form of footnotes to the text, appearing at the bottom of the page on which they are relevant; the advantage of this kind of note is that it does not interrupt the flow of the text but is immediately available on the page if needed. Such notes should be kept short, and few in number, as readers may tend to ignore a mass of small or close print below the main text. Footnotes are usually 'signposted' in the text by symbols such as the asterisk * or the dagger †, or by superscript numbers [1,2] (see example on page 1).

Quotations and references

It is valid, and often useful, to quote verbatim from or to refer to other publications — it shows awareness of work in the field and can add authority to a text. Before quoting, however, it is necessary to check whether the material is covered by copyright and needs the permission of the copyright-holder for quotation, with an acknowledgement for such permission being recorded in the report. Information on copyright may be found in Butcher (1981), Scarles (1980) and the *Writers' and artists' yearbook* (1984).

No permission is required merely to refer to a work. It is common practice to give a brief reference in the text and full details in a separate bibliographical section, using one of the recommended and standard forms (see page 17).

Illustrations

Some kinds of information are better presented in diagrammatic, pictorial or tabular form rather than as text. A sequence of events or the operation of a procedure or system, for example, may be much more clearly understood and absorbed when shown as a series of interlinked boxes or a flowchart, with arrows indicating direction, feedback or influence; similarly, a collection of numerical data becomes more significant when arranged in vertical and horizontal lines, with appropriate headings. The use of illustrations can also save space as well as achieve clarity; writers should familiarise themselves with the various forms and their particular suitabilities and exercise responsibility for selecting the best form for, and ensuring the relevance of, each illustration.

Among the most common illustrations are tables, pie charts, line graphs, bar graphs, pictograms, schematic and exploded diagrams, photographs (half-tones), surface charts, histograms, flowcharts, free-hand drawings and composite arrangements of text and ruled lines. Examples of some of these are shown here, (a) to (e), Fuller information and further examples can be found in Cooper (1964), Fletcher (1983), Gilchrist (1982), Mitchell (1974), Turk and Kirkman (1982) and Ward (1977).

(a) — **Pie Chart**

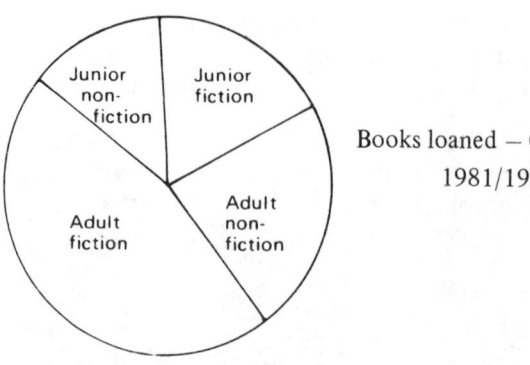

Books loaned — Central Library
1981/1982

(b) — Bar Graph

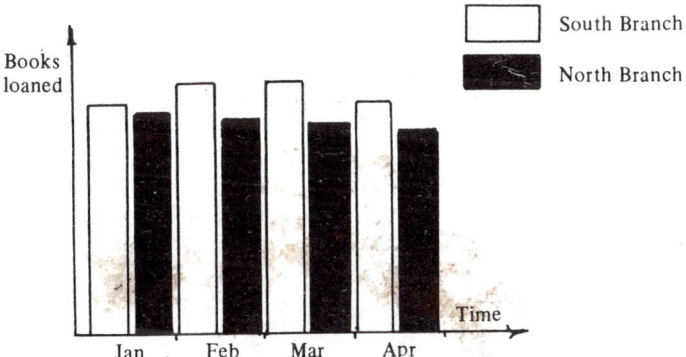

A bar chart is really a bar graph turned on its side: some libraries with large staffs use bar charts for timetabling.

(c) — Single & Multi-line Graphs

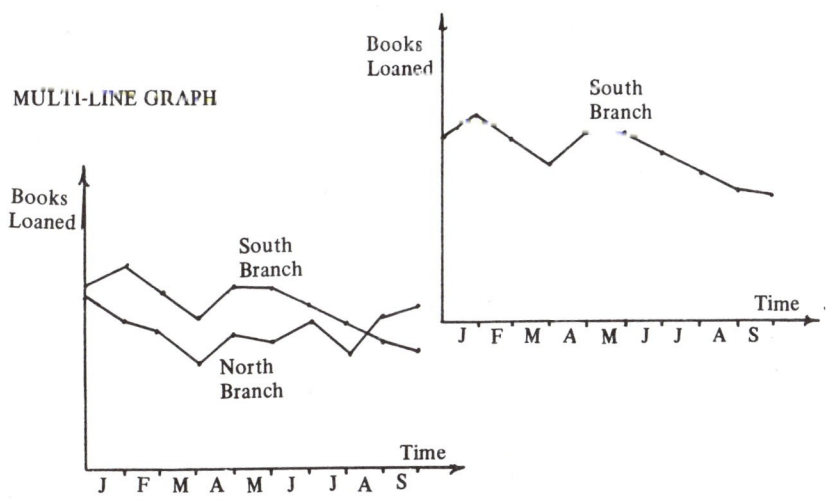

(d) — Dictionary File

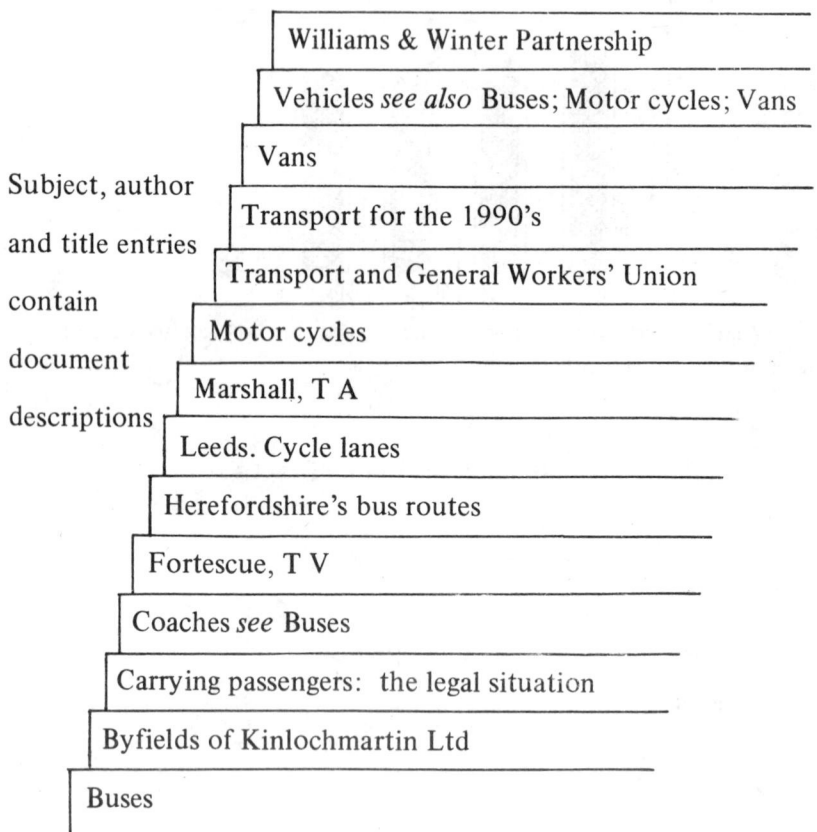

Subject, author and title entries contain document descriptions

- Williams & Winter Partnership
- Vehicles *see also* Buses; Motor cycles; Vans
- Vans
- Transport for the 1990's
- Transport and General Workers' Union
- Motor cycles
- Marshall, T A
- Leeds. Cycle lanes
- Herefordshire's bus routes
- Fortescue, T V
- Coaches *see* Buses
- Carrying passengers: the legal situation
- Byfields of Kinlochmartin Ltd
- Buses

(e) – THE BUDGETING CYCLE

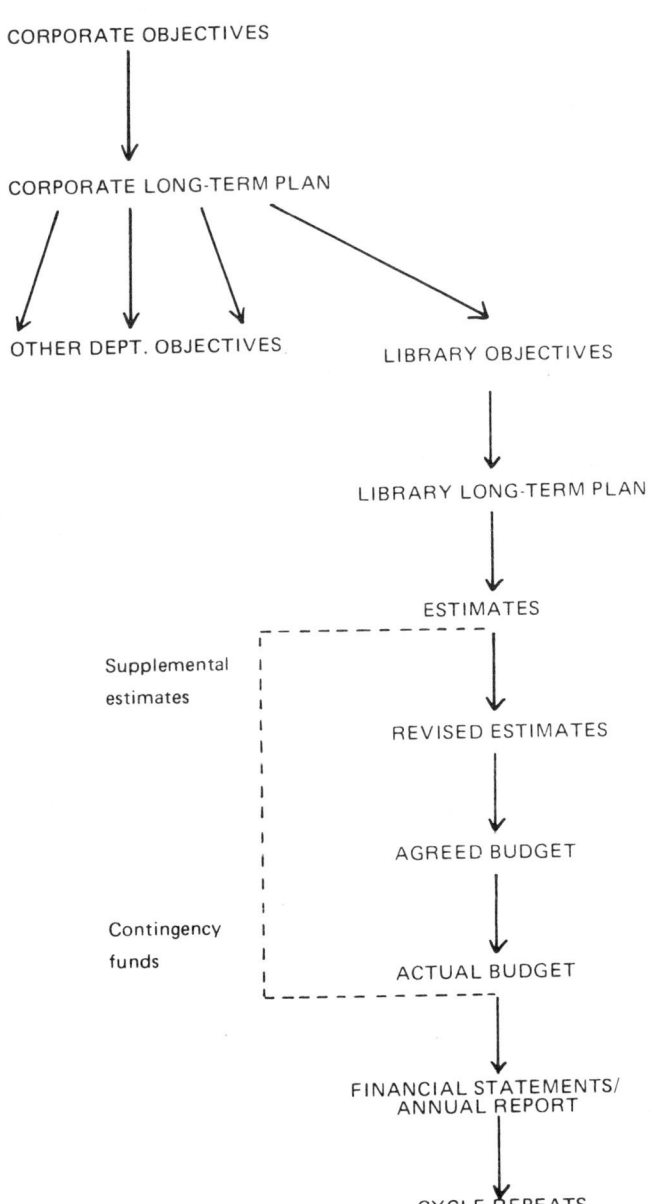

Tables are easily set out and need no particular expertise, but attention must be given to the correct alignment of the vertical and horizontal columns and to accuracy of calculation in 'totals'. Simple graphs and charts can be produced with basic tools such as pen and ruler; the completed illustration should, of course, clearly show the relevant units of measurement (months, £s, hundreds of items). Some artistic skill is required for the production of good diagrams of objects, but flowcharts can be drawn using a stencil containing the standard symbols.

If photographs are to be used — and these may be appropriate if particular importance is attached to 'actuality' — then a decision must be made as to whether multiple prints (matt or glossy) are to be produced and individually affixed in each copy of the report, or whether half-tones (produced as part of a printing or photocopying process) will be adequate — bearing in mind the loss of detail; this decision is likely to be influenced mainly by the required number of copies of the report.

Lettering in captions can be neatly written, typed, printed or produced by adhesive, transfer or stencil lettering sets available from stationers.

It is not always necessary to make an elaborate presentation of illustrations; a neat, straightforward display which either takes the place of text matter, or supplements it, is in most cases satisfactory. In publicity or marketing situations, where special funds may be earmarked for the production of an impressive publication, then full use may be made of colour, special papers, professional draughting, artistic, photographic and printing services.

The writer must also decide whether illustrations are to be placed alongside the text to which they relate (which makes them easy to see and quick to refer to, but may create layout and space difficulties) or to collect them in a separate illustrations section, perhaps in an appendix (which makes it easier to relate one illustration to another, but removes them from the relevant parts of the text). The pertinent question is whether the illustrations are essential to immediate comprehension of the text, or whether the text can be readily understood without them. In the latter case, the illustrations may be of interest only to a few readers wishing to investigate further and it may be acceptable, therefore, to supply them in a different physical format, such as microfiche, or to have them available on request.

Supplementary parts of the text

Glossary

It is sometimes necessary (see page 24) to use specialised vocabulary in a report, to convey precise meanings and avoid ambiguity, but this language may not be familiar to some readers; for their sake, definitions of terms, expansions of abbreviations and meanings of acronyms must be explained and may, if there are several instances within the text, be gathered together in an alphabetical glossary section. This is usually placed at the end of the main text, but can be located at the front to give a prior indication of the kind of vocabulary used and an opportunity for readers to scan the list before starting on the text itself. Authoritative sources should be checked to ensure that the correct definitions and expansions are listed.

Bibliographical references and further reading

As indicated on page 11, references to other works are frequently made in texts; whichever system of reference citation is used, the *full* bibliographical details of each reference must be given at some point. Sometimes the references for each chapter or section are gathered together at the end of that part; alternatively, they may be put into a single list at the end of the report (as in this publication). These bibliographical details may be used by readers as the basis for requesting copies from libraries or suppliers — it is therefore essential that the details given are complete and accurate, and set out consistently in one of the standard forms of presentation. It should not be assumed that, just because the writer knows what the 'Blue Book' and the 'BMJ' are, the readers will be equally knowledgeable, so full titles or approved abbreviated forms (see British Standards Institution (1970) BS 4148) should be used.

If the report is being prepared for publication as part of a series, or by a regular publisher, there may be a preferred or house style for the citation of other publications; this should be ascertained before the first reference is included in the text, so that the details may be provided in the correct form from the start.

Two common methods of citation in text are: i) giving the author's name and date of publication, as 'Marples (1980)', and ii) giving the author and a superscript running number, as 'Marples[1]'; in the first method, the full references are then listed in alphabetical order, while in the second they appear in order of the superscript numbers. Further details may be found in British Standards Institution (1976) BS 1629 and (1978) BS 5605, Butcher (1981) and Nicholas and Standley (1984).

A separate section of 'background' or 'further' or 'recommended' reading can also be included, to incorporate references to those publications which have not been specifically mentioned in the text, but which are thought relevant and useful to readers wishing to explore topics further.

Appendixes

Information which supplements the main text, or which has to be presented in a large block which would break up the text if inserted in it, can be placed in appendixes (or appendices) at the end of the report (before the index). Illustrations or a glossary might be treated in this way, or examples of standard forms or questionnaires, collections of statistical data and metric conversion tables.

The information contained in appendixes may be of a kind that will be consulted by only a few readers, but it should nevertheless be quickly retrievable and easily understood. Each appendix must be given a letter or number and an indicative title; these numbers or letters and titles are then used for reference in the text and in the contents list, thus adequately signalling the existence of the appendixes — otherwise the valuable information in them may remain unnoticed.

Acknowledgements

It has already been indicated (page 11) that acknowledgement for permission to reproduce copyright material must be given; it is usual (and polite) also to record thanks to individuals and organisations from whom assistance has been received (perhaps in the form of information, finance or research help) during the preparation of the report. Acknowledgements are generally placed before the main text.

Care should be taken to ensure that the acceptance of assistance from a particular source does not cast doubts upon the integrity or acceptability of the report's content.

Foreword and preface

It is not essential to provide a foreword or a preface for a report background or context can easily be included in the 'introduction' section of the main text. On occasion, however, the writer may wish to supply a more personal note on the background and this may form a preface; and sometimes, for publicity purposes or attribution of authority — it is helpful for a foreword to be written by someone other than the author (a well-known person in the subject field, for example).

Summary or abstract

Once the report has been completed, it is advisable to produce a summary (abstract) of the content; this can be included in the report, perhaps on the title page or on one of the preliminary pages, and acts both as an indicator of the content to those starting to read the report and as a reminder to those who have read it and wish to check quickly. Depending on the nature of the report, one or two or a few paragraphs may be needed. A further — and very common — use of a summary is its inclusion in abstracting periodicals and current awareness services, where it represents the report and brings it to the attention of a wider readership.

Summaries vary in form, some indicating in a general way what is to be found in the reports, others giving a distilled version of the content. The latter form is more useful if the summary is to be used independently of the report.

Readers of lengthy reports benefit from the provision of a summary at the beginning or end of each chapter or section, giving assistance in assimilating an argument or development.

Index

The majority of reports of the kind considered in this publication need an index; possible exceptions are those which are extremely short (covering one or two pages), and those which are self-indexing (with items arranged in alphabetical order, for example).

Writers must remember that although they know the text, its content and sequence, others do not. It is not sufficient to provide only a contents list, since its purpose is different from that of the index, the index giving comparatively detailed means of access to individual pages, paragraphs or lines in connection with specific topics.

The larger the report, the more detailed the index; readers cannot be expected to work their way through the whole report, or dip at random, in order to find a particular piece of information. The completed index comprises an alphabetical list (or lists) of subjects and names and the page, section or paragraph numbers in which those items appear. When there are several numbers against an index reference and the kind of information on the pages varies, it is useful to distinguish text from illustrative material, to indicate which is the major reference, and to show which references are to glossaries and to bibliographical citations; this can be done by devices such as underlining, typographical variation (bold, italic) or by abbreviations (ill., bib., gl.).

Before compiling an index for the first time, the writer should consult some of the works explaining the technique of indexing and prescribing standards, such as Anderson (1971), Booth and South (1982), British Standards Institution (1976) BS 3700, Butcher (1981) and Knight (1979). Following the recommendations given therein, a respectable index can be compiled, in which all significant concepts are included, using the terms likely to be sought by readers as well as the terminology of the text. The index should cover not only the main text but also the preliminary pages, appendixes and other sections if they are judged to include sought terms and specifically desired information. Authors not willing (or able) to compile their own indexes should consult the list of professional indexers published by the Society of Indexers (1984).

One decision to be made concerning the index (and any other part of the report in which information is to be alphabetically arranged) is whether the order is to be 'word-by-word' or 'letter-by-letter'; either order is acceptable, but the same order must be used consistently throughout a particular report. In word-by-word order 'Public telephones' comes before 'Publicity' (because 'Public' as a word precedes 'Publicity' as a word; in letter-by-letter order 'Publicity' comes before 'Public telephones' (because 'publici. . .' comes before 'Public t. . .' and the space between 'Public' and 'telephones' is ignored. Conventions also exist regarding the filing of numbers and symbols; filing rules are explained in the references given above and in British Standards Institution (1969) BS 1749. It should be noted that if word processors or computers are used for the compilation of indexes, they may have their own individual sets of filing rules – these should be checked, as they may not be what the writer expects or wants.

List of illustrations

If there are more than just one or two illustrations, and it is likely that they will need to be referred to on their own, a list of illustrations, showing numbers, captions and page references, should be compiled. This precedes the main text. Separate lists of diagrams, photographs and tables may be preferred, if there are many.

Title page

The importance of the title page should not be overlooked. Some reports are produced with covers which sometimes double as title pages, but whether or not a cover is used, the necessary information to identify the document must appear on a title page of some kind. The information needed consists of the title (including subtitle), name(s) of the author(s), name and full address of the publisher and the date of publication (frequently forgotten on amateurish publications, but essential for placing the report in context); in addition, names of organisations involved in sponsorship of the report, name and number within a certain series of publications, name and address of printer, copyright information and ISBN* (International Standard Book Number) may be included. Number) may be included.

---

* If the report is to be formally published and generally available, there can be an advantage in obtaining an ISBN from the Standard Book Numbering Agency; this constitutes a unique identifier for the publication and assists in ordering and acquisition by booksellers and libraries. Details are given in the *Writers' and artists' yearbook* (1984).

Contents list

This should be the last part of the report to be prepared; writers should resist the temptation to compile it before the full and final text, with all its preliminaries and supplementary sections, has been put together. The aim of the contents list is to show the sections into which the report is divided and on which pages they start; the chapter or section headings and the relevant page numbers must therefore be accurate, and this can only be ensured when the list is compiled from the final copy, since headings and page numbers typically undergo several changes during the course of preparation.

The list should include preliminaries such as preface, foreword, summary and list of illustrations as well as items like glossaries, lists of references, appendixes and indexes. All sections should, of course, be listed in the order in which they appear in the report; normally the first page number of each section is given, but it can sometimes be useful to give the full extent of the pages taken up by each section.

CHAPTER 4 : STYLE, LANGUAGE AND TONE

This publication has already stressed the importance of using the 'right' style, language and tone when preparing a report; what is more difficult is to say exactly how this is to be done. Writers must develop a sensitivity to the meanings of words, the effects of placing words in a particular order, and the nuances and connotations carried by their phrases and sentences, and must be aware of the potential effects (some desired, some unwanted) of their compositions upon readers. For this reason, writing reports is best done with plenty of time to spare for consideration of what is provisionally put down, for assessment, revision and reassessment; this ideal cannot always be achieved, but it is imperative that, at the least, the final draft be read through in an attempt to catch the serious errors and misconstructions.

Some writers wish — and feel it appropriate — to express something of their own personalities in their styles and choices of language; it is important to remember that they also thereby stimulate some kind of response in their readers (perhaps boredom, or sarcasm, or antipathy). It may be better to act cautiously and to employ a generally acceptable style and vocabulary (unless the writers are very sure of their readers). In report writing, the result should be 'user-friendly', assisting comprehension, not getting in the way by being too obvious and contrived.

It is, unfortunately, easy to lose the goodwill of some readers by using words, expressions, forms and constructions which they do not like, or which they claim are wrong. Language, its expression and usage are always in a state of change, with new words and phrases and grammatical forms arriving and, after a period, being absorbed into the 'approved' varieties of language for spoken and written communication; problems can arise when individual perceptions of what is acceptable vary.

Writers should therefore make full use of dictionaries (for meaning and spelling) and of the range of guides to 'good English' which includes Fowler (1965), Gowers (1973), Oxford guide (1983),

Partridge (1963) and Wood (1981), among others. The aim, as always, is to achieve clarity and interest and to make the content flow. To this end, attention should be paid in particular to vocabulary, spelling, grammar, punctuation and tone.

VOCABULARY

Most writers know, at the time of writing, the kind of readers their reports are likely to have, even if they do not know them individually; they may be colleagues, members of a committee or association, college tutors, managers at a higher level, junior staff or members of any other category. This helps in the choice of language 'level' — particularly if the readers have similar characteristics — and in the selection of terms to be used, which can be important in creating a first impression, as too low a level can irritate, while one which is too complicated can put readers off before they have started to absorb the substance of the report. Written communications are more interesting when a full range of vocabulary is employed — and writers will find Crabb (1916), Nuttall (1979) and Roget (1982) useful for suggesting synonyms and alternative forms ; the words chosen should be those which the majority of readers will recognise, however, rather than abstruse and little-known forms. Sexist and racist language and examples must of course be avoided; NALGO (1983) and Miller and Swift (1981) give guidance on the former.

Special, technical language

Care should be exercised in the use of words which have specialised meanings particular to the field of information work. Obviously, words which refer precisely to the relevant concepts must be employed; what is contemptuously regarded as 'jargon' is often the exact vocabulary needed to refer unambiguously to a set of related concepts. In documents relating to information work terms such as 'acquisition', 'recall', 'file', 'store', 'database', 'issue', 'bibliography' and 'memory' will be encountered. If writers are sure of their readers' familiarity with such terms, there may be no need for any further explanation; but if not (and in a specialised field this is often the case) then elaboration is essential, either in the text (in parenthesis or as a footnote) or in a separate glossary of terms (see page 17). Writers using newly coined words or recently formed acronyms (words formed from initial letters of other words), or words which are familiar but have acquired new meanings must amplify them in a similar way.

A further difficulty is that even within the information work field a particular term can be used with more than one meaning, dependent upon the specific context. 'Circulation' in a public library refers to the issue of items from stock on loan to borrowers, while in a company setting it indicates the movement of periodicals (journals, magazines) around predetermined circulation lists of readers. Similarly, 'bibliography', 'file', 'issue', 'charge', 'store' and 'catalogue' all have more than one meaning.

For people outside the information field, or new to it (such as company managers nominally responsible for information services, or lay persons on public library committees), the vocabulary can be confusing, since words from the everyday language — 'accession', 'terminal', 'reserve', 'network', 'node', 'package' and 'trapping', for instance — take on entirely different meanings. When the understanding and cooperation of such people is needed, the writer must assist their comprehension by explanation of terms in this category.

Plain English

Some writers are tempted not only to use a full vocabulary, but to employ longer words rather than shorter and to produce complicated sentences. The Plain English Campaign, launched in 1979, has found that many people are confused by writing of this kind, particularly in official communications, and is working to improve their use and comprehensibility. The emphasis of the Campaign's work is to use straightforward means of expressing messages and to reduce the use of long words and phrases which mask the true meaning rather than enhance it. Cutts and Maher (1980) give examples of what to avoid and how to assist comprehension of written information, and Turk and Kirkman (1982), Cooper (1964), and Ashe (1981), among other authors on the art of writing, set out Gunning's 'Fog Index' formula (based on the number of words of more than three syllables in a text, together with the average number of words in a sentence) which writers may like to use to check their texts for readability.

The use, merely for effect, of foreign words and phrases should be avoided; some readers may not understand them and others may be irritated by them. Words, originally from other languages, which have been absorbed into everyday use and are readily understood, having no English equivalent, are acceptable.

Repetition

To repeat something already stated may be regarded as wasteful, unnecessary and boring, but there are occasions when it can serve to emphasise a point and remind the reader. In this case the repeated content may be best placed in a later section and phrased in a different way. Repetition can also bring to the reader's attention something missed the first time it was mentioned — the amount of concentration readers give to documents varies according to mood, health, ambient temperature, time of day and other influences, and repeating important matter can help to compensate for this.

SPELLING, GRAMMAR, PUNCTUATION

As with vocabulary, there are many pitfalls to be avoided when it comes to spelling, ordering, punctuating and capitalising words and phrases. Reference should be made to dictionaries and to guides such as Butcher (1981), Carey (1971), Hart's rules (1983) and those already mentioned on pages 23 & 24, so that current accepted practice may be followed. Whenever alternative spellings are permitted — like 'organisation, organization' — one must be selected and used consistently; sometimes a publisher's house style may determine the choice, but otherwise it is the writer's responsibility — and particular care should be taken when more than one contributor to a report is involved, to ensure that both (or all) are using the same spelling. Slight differences between British and American spelling should be noted (colour/color, sulphur/sulfur, catalogue/catalog, aluminium/aluminum) and appropriate amendment made.

TONE

It is easy for a writer inadvertently to imbue a text with personal feelings or attitudes experienced at the time of preparation —

boredom, impatience, resentment, anxiety, frustration or excitement, for instance; because this may have an adverse effect on readers, it is wise to try to write in a more detached frame of mind. Similarly, the use of humour and irony should normally be avoided, as these can be misunderstood or even cause offence. However, it can sometimes be beneficial to indicate some personal enthusiasm in what is presented, to show that the writer is not totally indifferent to the outcome; and if the report is restricted in distribution to a group of known colleagues or members, then it is likely that any lighthearted touches shown in the text will be correctly interpreted.

The overall tone of a report will be influenced by the nature of its message and the kind of relationship and attitudes which exist between the writer and the recipients; on the final reading of the text, before it goes for reproduction, the writer should assess whether the effect on readers will be what was originally intended.

CHAPTER 5 : COPY PREPARATION AND REPRODUCTION

The degree of control which authors have over the physical appearance, format and production of their reports varies. The writer should be interested and involved in decisions made in this connection, but may not be the best person to make solo choices, not necessarily having design and copy reproduction expertise. Advice should be sought from specialist individuals and publications, so as to produce the optimum result.

An author working within an organisation is likely to have access at least to professional typing and copying facilities and in a large enterprise this may extend to a full range of dictating, typewriting, typesetting, printing, photographic and reproduction capabilities. The best plan is to find out (before starting to write the report) what is readily available, what it can do and how much it will cost, and then to choose what comes within the appropriate economic limits and what is going to produce the 'best' result within those limits (in terms of numbers of copies, speed of production, quality and so on), bearing in mind always the effect which it is desired to have on the report's readers.

Individuals working on their own and having no mechanical aids may feel themselves at a considerable disadvantage, but are still capable of producing effective and presentable documents. A handwritten report must be prepared with particular care, as manuscript which is difficult to read can obscure an otherwise significant contribution; the judicious use of spacing, underlining, capitalisation and other devices can improve legibility and visual appeal. If at all possible, though, a typewritten document should be produced, perhaps by hiring a machine or coming to an arrangement with a friend or colleague who will type from a manuscript.

The final version of the report which the author produces is – in the simplest production procedure – the actual master from which copies are made for distribution; in more complex systems, it is copied from by a typist, word processor operator or typesetter who produces a properly laid out and styled end-product. The remaining sections of this chapter apply, in some measure, to any method of production — though the order in which matters are attended to in practice may vary.

SIZE AND LENGTH

No optimum size or length can be recommended for all circumstances, but the finished product should be convenient to handle and to read and have a 'balanced' look. The international paper sizes A5 (210 x 148 mm) — like this book — and A4 (297 x 210 mm) are commonly used; commercial publishers employ also a traditional range of sizes for their publications — see British Standards Institution (1970) BS1413 and Butcher (1981).

The number of pages in the final report is influenced by the number of words in the text, the number and length of supplementary sections, the paper size and the style and size of type used; certain types of binding and securing also place restrictions on the number of pages which can be accommodated (see page 32). If the report is to be sent through the post to recipients, the cost of this is directly related to the size and weight.

In the case of student project reports and others which are required for formal assessment, the length is sometimes limited by regulation (between 5,000 and 6,000 words, for example); the number of pages taken up then varies according to the method of copy preparation and reproduction.

LAYOUT

Any written document intended for others to read should be presented in an agreeable layout. Pages crowded with closely-spaced, small print, with no headings or other 'signposts', are either intimidating or tedious and, in the case of a report whose recipients may not be enthusiastic readers to start with, the effect can be deadening. The formal structure (see pages 8 & 9) of the report should therefore be reflected in the layout, with distinct headings, plenty of white space around and between paragraphs, adequate margins (top, bottom and sides), helpful use of indentation (starting and ending lines further in from the margins) and variation in style and size of lettering.

Illustrations, whether placed in the text or in a separate section (see page 16), must be clearly captioned and identified by number and given enough space so that they can be comfortably inspected; if possible, they should be vertically placed on the page, but if a horizontal placing is necessary, the illustration should be positioned so that the top is at the left of the page. Butcher (1981) and Hart's rules (1983) give further information on the preparation of illustrations for printing.

There should be no doubt where each section of the report begins and ends, and appendixes should be individually identified and clearly separated from the main text. The layout of the index may differ from that of the rest of the report, with the entries listed in two (or more) columns; this is possible if the individual entries are short, and can help to reduce the total number of pages.

Typographical variation and devices

For highlighting significant passages or data, and for distinguishing one section from another, full use should be made of whatever means of lettering variation is available. Handwritten copy can include underlining, capital letters, differences in size, and whatever decoration the writer feels able competently to produce. Use of a typewriter permits additional kinds of decoration and framing and, with the more sophisticated models, changes of type style, size and pitch (number of characters per inch) are possible; this allows words, paragraphs or whole sections to be set in *italic* or **bold** for emphasis. The ultimate in variety and text manipulation may be available to some writers, through word processing or printing equipment – but such facilities are by no means essential for the production of a good-looking report.

THE 'MASTER' COPY

A writer whose handwritten 'best' copy is to be used for direct reproduction of other copies needs to check that it is clean, distinct and correct before generating further copies from it. If carbon copies for distribution are produced simultaneously with the top copy, they must be checked for clarity and for smudges (some types of carbon paper are worse than others in this respect) and any corrections made on the top copy must be transferred onto them.

If the writer's final version goes to a typist or other professional operator for reformatting, it must be correct, clear and unambiguous, with all requirements for spacing, style and headings indicated so that there can be no doubt in the operator's mind what is wanted; this avoids delay in production and errors which need correction at a later stage. No major changes should be made once the final version has been passed on by the author. The complete typed or printed 'proof' then goes to the author for checking; this must be done with great care, to make sure that every letter, space and punctuation mark is as indicated in the original. Any discrepancies found are marked and the proof returned for correction; there is a set of standard marks for the correction of proofs — see British Standards Institution (1976) BS 5261C, *Writers' and artists' yearbook* (1984) and Butcher (1981). Those corrections are then checked; this final checking is important, since it is possible for new errors to occur during the correction of earlier ones.

The final draft of the entire report should be completely read through, checking for comprehensibility, completeness, consistency, logical development, accuracy of spelling, grammar and punctuation; references in the text should match with those in the bibliographical sections and illustrations and appendixes appear in the correct sequence. If there has been any rewriting or change in sequence of sections, or removal of any material, this must be reflected in the contents list. Title page information should be checked for accuracy and completeness — it may be not until this stage that the final title is confirmed and added, together with the date. The index may also be completed at this point, since the final page numbers are now known.

A report published with noticeable errors or with sloppy presentation engenders doubts about the reliability of its content as a whole — it pays, therefore, to attend to faults before production of multiple copies begins.

PRODUCTION OF MULTIPLE COPIES

The chosen means of producing copies for distribution and their physical form depends on what facilities are available to the author, the number of copies required, the speed with which they are wanted, the standard and quality of reproduction needed, and the cost. The expected life of the report should also be considered; if the publication is likely to be discarded shortly after distribution, because of its ephemeral interest, it is extravagant (and irresponsible) to produce high-cost, hard-wearing copies with top-quality paper and print and with stout binding. On the other hand, if it is a document which will be relevant and in demand and stored in information centres for many years, then such copies can be justified.

As indicated earlier, a few carbon copies may be produced at the same time as the master copy, giving quick, low-cost results; in some situations low-quality flimsy copies of this kind are quite satisfactory. If larger numbers are required, they can be produced by photocopying, either on site within the organisation, through a commercial printing and copying service, or on a machine located in a public building such as a library or post office. Costs charged for copies vary considerably and so it is worth checking several sources and comparing costs before selecting one. If full-scale commercial printing is utilised, comparative costs and production times should be checked, after full details of requirements have been supplied to the printers; size, colour and weight of paper, face, style and size of type, and cover details all have to be chosen and samples approved. Individuals and groups producing reports on a self-publishing basis can find useful advice in Treweek and Zeitlyn (1983), Smith (1980) and Ward and Ward (1979).

If money and time permit, it is worth considering the use of such features as tinted papers for different sections of the report, stiff dividers between sections, tabbed or thumb-indexed pages, pockets in covers to hold additional publicity material or inserts like maps, plans or microfiche copies of supplementary data. These, if well designed, can add to the visual appeal of the publication and — if appropriate — help to sell copies.

BINDING

Several methods exist for the securing and protection of copies; the choice is influenced by those factors mentioned in the preceding section.

For some reports, containing only a few pages, stapling across the left-hand corner and insertion in a plastic wallet (transparent so that the title page or cover information shows through) may be adequate. Other, larger, documents may be more suitable for spiral binding — plastic or wire inserted by machine through holes punched in the edges of the pages; ring binders can be used (bought from stationers), the pages of the report being punched at the edge and inserted in the binder, which can then be labelled on the front and spine. Other forms include glueing the edges of the pages and fixing into the spine of a fabric, card or plastic cover, sliding the pages into a plastic channel, stapling into stiff covers, inserting into spring-backed binders, as well as full commercial stitching and casing in 'hardback' form. Authors having responsibility for the binding of copies should find out what is available within their organisations, from printing and binding suppliers and services, and from stationers, and select the most suitable method. Periodicals dealing with office and business organisation are helpful in the identification of types and suppliers of apparatus.

CHAPTER 6 : REPORTS FOR PARTICULAR PURPOSES

The principles and suggestions set out in previous chapters are intended to apply to reports of all kinds. This chapter seeks to identify the particular emphases or characteristics to be considered in relation to individual types of reports. They are not exclusive, but rather overlap with each other, suggesting merely a frame within which a specific report may be viewed at the start.

STUDENT PROJECT REPORTS

As part of their education for information work, students are frequently required to carry out projects, using the appropriate investigative methods (questionnaire, interview, literature survey) and to produce reports on them. The reports are then checked and graded, to contribute to the overall schemes of assessment for the courses. Marks are, typically, awarded for content, method and physical presentation.

Guidelines setting out the precise requirements for the project and the report are normally given to the students (either in writing or orally) by the course directorate, and include instructions about choice of topic, expected length, recommended sources and methods, physical presentation, nature of permitted supplementary material, number of copies required, the procedure for assessment, the number or percentage of marks available and timetable for submission. Students should familiarise themselves with requirements before starting work on their projects, as failure to comply with them may place their final grade in jeopardy.

Unlike many report writers, students preparing projects are in the fortunate position of being able (and being expected to) choose their own topics and to ask for advice and support from their tutors, to whom any doubts about requirements, topics, methods and format should be referred, The situation is also unusual in that all concerned are united in wanting the report to be a success, therefore working towards this aim should be unproblematic, providing the requisite amount of effort and care is put into the task.

A certain number of words is usually specified ('not more than 5,000', 'between 4,000 and 6,000, not including supplementary data'); this is intended as a guide — a couple of hundred words under or over the limit need not be of concern. It is not necessary to count every word in the report; an average, taken over a few representative pages and then multiplied by the total number of pages, gives a reasonable estimate.

General instructions on binding often say no more than 'a suitable cover must be used'; the purpose here is to (a) identify, (b) enhance and (c) protect the report and so a clearly labelled wallet folder, ring binder, plastic pocket or stapled card cover (all obtainable from stationers and some campus shops) can be used, without great expense being incurred. More specific requirements (for size, hard covers, uniform labelling and lettering, type of fixing) should be observed; services are sometimes provided on campus or by local firms.

PROFESSIONAL AND PERSONAL DEVELOPMENT REPORTS

These may be required in at least two different contexts. The first relates to those involved in the Library Association's qualification process to become Chartered Librarians. Licentiates wishing to apply for election to Associateship must submit written reports on the work carried out during a specified period of service, giving an account of the work which they have been involved in, a self-assessment in terms of professional development and an evaluation of the work of the information environments concerned.

The specification for the report (length and presentation) is laid down by the Library Association; candidates should obtain this (Library Association, 1984), take account of the requirements and keep up to date with further announcements.

The second context is that of an employee who, as part of the personnel management procedure in an organisation, is required to submit, perhaps at annual intervals, a report on personal progress throughout that period. The specification for this context is likely to be less formal, but may still require presentation in prescribed sections on a standard form.

In both these cases the emphasis is on presentation of self in the best possible light, therefore events and situations need to be selected which highlight achievement, responsibility, teamwork, originality, competence, capability, initiative or whatever other quality the individual feels important. Less advantageous factors should not be ignored, since they can be utilised to indicate learning from experience, increased awareness, willingness to take responsibility for one's mistakes, ideas for remedy, a sense of realism and so on. Care needs to be taken when handling comments which may be seen as derogatory as far as others are concerned, since these may become known to a wider circle than intended, and may redound to the detriment of the writer — in any case, it can look as though one wishes always to blame others for errors.

DEPARTMENTAL ACTIVITY PROGRESS REPORTS

These may be required as part of an organisation's management process, so that the activities of each part can be monitored and coordinated; periods covered vary, depending on the nature of the activity, the degree to which it fluctuates from week to week or year to year and the extent to which organisational policy and routine are affected as a result. In each case, the writer should — as usual — identify the major purpose, and also any useful by-products which may be achieved. What is of interest is likely to arise from a comparison of reports over a particular period, by identifying changes, their underlying causes and effects. Sometimes such reports are a useful means of notifying and recording trends or unusual events and indicating new needs. In other circumstances, all that is required is a return of numerical data (number of loans, percentage of database entries updated, sickness and accident totals), though even here it is advisable to add a footnote to explain an abnormally high or low total, or to add that a separate report is being prepared on a particular issue, for further discussion or action.

It should be remembered that information included for this kind of report, when made available generally, may be used at a later stage for purposes other than that for which it was originally intended, therefore the interpretation of data must be clear, with little opportunity for misunderstanding.

RESEARCH REPORTS

'Research' is used here in the sense of 'critical study or investigation'. Many, perhaps most, such reports are produced subsequent to the granting of funds by an organisation to an individual or group of individuals, or to another organisation, to look into a particular subject and produce an account of the findings. Such a grant normally has, as one of its conditions, that a report or reports must be produced within a given time, sometimes at specified stages during the research process, sometimes only when the work has been completed.

What is needed in these cases is an initial review of the 'state of the art' (what was known about the subject at the commencement of the research), the particular aspects which this research investigated and the background to it, the methods employed to discover the 'facts', the findings, and some conclusions or proposals. Even if very little is discovered, or if the current research merely confirms what was already known, or if the research is inconclusive, this must still be stated in a report; future investigators may continue from this point. Unusual or unexplained phenomena can be recorded, perhaps in appendixes, and suggestions made for further work. Moore (1983) gives information on research methods.

MEETINGS REPORTS

There are two common cases of meetings reports. First, those prepared by volunteers undertaking the recording of the activity of occasional and probably informal meetings and the circulation of that record to all the participants. The importance here is that the names of those attending, any agreements or decisions reached, results of votes taken and so on, must be recorded in an acceptable and unequivocal way, so that they may be forwarded to all those affected and be available for consultation at a later stage. A plain, photocopied report of one or two pages is often all that is required.

The second case, more formal, is that of regular meetings of bodies such as committees, societies and clubs, where the recording of the meetings' progress is the responsibility of the permanent secretary. The records (usually known as 'minutes') become part of the official records of the body concerned and may have some legal or authoritative force.

Absolute accuracy and faithfulness to the conduct of the meeting are required and the minutes of the meeting are usually read out at, or circulated before, the following meeting, for confirmation by the body as a whole. There are a number of generally accepted conventions regarding the conduct and recording of this formal kind of meeting, and those in secretarial positions in bodies of these types should consult one of the publications on the subject, such as Quinn (1982).

ANNUAL REPORTS

Many organisations (societies, library boards and committees, for example) produce, both for publicity purposes and for monitoring, reports of their activities and progress over the past year — sometimes for presentation to members and discussion at an annual general meeting. The emphasis here is on letting the recipients know, or reminding them, what has happened during the past year, and perhaps on giving an account of the handling of finances. Relevant data must be carefully gathered, nothing must be omitted in which the readership may be interested, and it must be presented in a form which (if reader involvement is genuinely to be encouraged) creates and enhances interest. A standard format, with similar headings from year to year ('Membership', 'Publications', 'Training'), is useful for comparison, but on the other hand may lose interest after a while. Physical appearance and design may be important in this case.

SYSTEM EVALUATION REPORTS

Three examples of situations in which this kind of report may be required are

i) an investigation to discover which, out of several systems or pieces of equipment, is most suitable for a particular application

ii) a testing — on a pilot project basis — of an apparatus or system which it is intended to employ on a large scale, or with multiple applications, if the initial operation is deemed worthwhile, and

iii) an enquiry into the cause of failures in an existing operational system.

On occasion a whole series of reports may be generated, following the investigation, choice, pilot testing and full implementation of the system.

The purpose of these reports is usually, in situations (i) and (ii), to inform all those who are concerned in selection, implementation and utilisation about the requirements of the application, the criteria by which the systems should be judged, the features of available systems, data on their performance in the field and recommendations or conclusions about the best course of action; and in situation (iii), to identify faults and find solutions. In addition, the reports often perform a very useful service to others, at a later time, who are entering upon the same field of investigation in relation to their specific needs — published reports thus enable these investigators to benefit from the work done for earlier surveys.

With regard to the technical information which is almost certain to be part of this kind of report, there may be some 'field-specific' terminology which, for the sake of precision and exactness, must be employed, but it should not pass without explanation if there is any chance that the readers of the report may not be familiar with it. Explanation may take the form of supplementary text, footnotes, a glossary, or illustrations; as noted on page 12, an illustration — if in a well-chosen form — can make a principle or procedure immediately clear in circumstances where additional words would only confuse. Linked illustrations, for example in which one flowchart ends with a box which becomes the first step in the following chart, can provide an easily comprehended 'picture' of a system — frequently with no necessity for readers to understand the technical processes which are involved. It may be appropriate to include photographs (perhaps those provided by manufacturers), though it is best to use them only when they show an important feature or quality (such as comparative size), or when a well-placed and interesting example can lighten an otherwise heavy section of the report.

It is important to remember, when tempted to use data supplied by manufacturers or suppliers, that their interest lies in selling (renting, leasing) new systems and that they therefore take a consistently optimistic view of the systems' performance. An evaluation report by an independent, detached or disinterested investigator should aim at compensating for this and 'tell it as it really is'. Only then can informed judgements be made.

In the 'fault-finding' report, there is frequently some urgency, and therefore the writing may have to be executed in haste. A structure worked out at the start ('problem', 'method of investigation', 'possible causes', 'recommendations') is especially helpful in this situation.

PERSONNEL REPORTS, PERFORMANCE APPRAISAL REPORTS

These may be related to the departmental progress reports dealt with earlier (page 36) and are concerned more with the personal progress, performance and development of individuals than with the department as a whole. Some organisations require these to be submitted on a regular basis (say, annually) and link them to salary reviews and promotion structures. Practices differ markedly – some organisations regarding such reports as confidential to the people who write them and to the personnel department, while others make copies available to the individuals who are the subject of the reports, for comment.

Whatever the actual practice in any organisation, it is wise to assume that these reports are not (and cannot be) given the highest level of confidential treatment – several people tend to be involved in the preparation, handling, reproduction and filing of organisational papers. What is recorded, therefore, should be carefully thought out, accurate in every detail and with a complete absence of mischief or malice. Unguarded or easily misunderstood comments which are officially filed can damage a staff member's progress and reputation.

Sometimes a structure is prescribed by a standard printed form – an example is given in Ritchie (1982) – while elsewhere the report may take whatever form the writer wishes. In those cases where the persons who are the subjects of the reports see them and are invited to comment, writers should consider, while preparing the documents, what those comments may be – this may influence the style and tone used. In the course of such consideration, writers may come to recognise their own qualities, faults and performance deficits and perhaps reach an altered perspective of their colleagues.

FINANCIAL REPORTS

These may be, for example, treasurers' annual reports relating to societies or clubs, forecasts of or demands for funding (budgets) for a forthcoming period, comparisons of actual expenditure with that of previous periods or with budgeted expenditure, showing variances. In each case, there is likely to be a standard format, dictated either by custom and habit or by a prescribed organisational form; Blagden (1982) and Peters (1980) give further information.

The report for a society should include for a specified period (usually twelve months) a) the income and expenditure account, showing details of expenditure analysed under expense headings, sums received — also suitably analysed, and either a surplus of income over expenditure or a deficit, when expenditure exceeds income, and b) the balance sheet, showing what the current position is with regard to assets and liabilities. Footnotes, or notes on a separate sheet, should be added if it is felt necessary to explain unusual or extraordinary items which might give rise to query by the membership. The treasurer's report is normally accompanied by a report by the society's auditors.

Forecasts and demands should give an indication as to the basis of calculations, how much has been included for inflation, whether such items as overhead expenditure have been included and exactly how money will be spent. Most organisations have their own standard format for the presentation of this information; however it is presented, amounts must be clearly expressed and attributed to named items, columns must be totalled accurately and notes appended to explain unusual features.

Reports which compare the costs of one period with those of another must take into consideration differences in the basis of calculation (has the percentage for postage always been included, for instance) and necessary explanatory information added. Unless such differences and notes are highlighted, readers will assume that the figures for any two periods can be compared on the same basis and this may lead to misunderstanding and faulty decision making.

ACCOMMODATION SURVEYS

Reports are sometimes required on the current state of usage of the accommodation in a building or on a site, to include suggestions for possible new extensions, or for improving efficiency and effectiveness. These practically always need to have a significant number of illustrations, particularly plans, showing present usage of rooms and floors, direction of traffic movement through the building, and proposed changes. If professional help for the production of plans is not available, satisfactory results can be achieved by the competent use of graph paper, careful measurement (of rooms, furniture, equipment, corridors), and the use of coloured pens and stickers. Data may be needed on the average number of people per room, space per person, number of hours per week for which rooms are in occupation and so on; this should be presented in easily understood form. Questionnaires may be used to obtain staff input to the survey and a copy of each should be included — perhaps as an appendix.

CHAPTER 7 : LAUNCHING THE REPORT
– AND AFTERWARDS

The actual task of report writing may be over when the copies are produced, but the author's responsibility does not always stop at that point.

The ways in which the reports get to their intended recipients depend on the circumstances in which they were generated. In an organisation, regular internal reports such as progress reports are often distributed to a standard list of names via the internal mailing systems and for externally distributed copies the postal service is usually employed. Individuals or small groups who have produced reports which they wish to send to a selection of people need to choose the best method for promoting and delivering their work.

Consideration should be given to advance notification of the report's appearance – this can be useful in generating an atmosphere of anticipation – but the report itself must be substantial and significant enough, in that case, to fulfil expectations. Prior notice – by phone call or letter, or by advertisement – of the forthcoming publication is useful also in warning recipients who are on a distribution list that something is coming which requires their attention or will catch their interest. It is possible, in an informal manner, also to pass on background information which does not appear in the report, or to lessen the impact of 'bad news' by indicating that 'things have already started to improve'.

By publication day, names and addresses of recipients should be known, checked for accuracy and listed, and envelopes, wrappers or labels prepared. Special posting arrangements should have been fixed with the post office or with the organisation's despatch department, a choice made between first-class and second-class post and consideration given to the inclusion of reply cards for comment (perhaps prepaid). The cost of distribution should, of course, have been included in any estimates for the cost of producing the report.

Sometimes it is quite sufficient for the report to be sent out on its own, without any accompaniments, but more often it is helpful (and adds to the general good impression which may be sought) to enclose it with a compliments slip or letter, indicating the sender and perhaps the circumstances from which the report arises or other background information, and inviting comments by bringing particular sections to the readers' attention. Such letters may be reproduced in multiple copies with no personal message, or may be standard but with individual names and comments inserted; if a word processor is available, the matching of standard letters with lists of names and addresses is easily performed. Advice on writing letters is given in James (1983), Saville and Saville (1981) and Turk and Kirkman (1982). In some cases a standard form or covering note may have to be attached — for a student project report or a professional development report — and in this case the regulations or requirements should be observed. It is sometimes necessary for the signature of the author to appear either on the document or on the accompanying paper; in any case the personal name, telephone number and address of someone responsible should appear prominently so that readers may make contact if further enquiry or comment is desired. Statements dissociating an organisation from the content are sometimes required, with an indication that what follows is the author's personal opinion, not a formal statement of policy.

ORAL PRESENTATION

Organisational situations sometimes demand that a written report, submitted to a committee or other group, be orally presented to the members. In this case, the content of the presentation depends upon whether the written document has been circulated beforehand in order to give members the time to read it. If so, the presenter may assume that at least some of the members will have a degree of familiarity with the content, and so should concentrate on talking about the report, giving background, highlighting particular points, summarising implications and inviting questions; if the report is not distributed until the time of the meeting itself, then the presenter should give a brief summary, stressing problems, solution and conclusion aspects, while perhaps asking members to consult certain pages for illustration. What the presenter should *not* do is to read through the report word for word, since this adds nothing to what the members already have in their hands.

Most reports receive at least some comment and authors should endeavour to get feedback (formal and informal) on their work; from this, and from the knowledgeable perusal of reports written by others, the technique of report writing may be developed and refined.

REFERENCES

ANDERSON, M.D. (1971) *Book indexing* Cambridge University Press.

ASHE, Geoffrey. (1981) *The art of writing made simple.* Heinemann.

BLAGDEN, J. (1982) *Financial management. In*: Handbook of special librarianship and information work. 5th ed. Editor: L.J. Anthony. Aslib. (Ch. 4).

BOOTH, Pat F. and SOUTH, M.L. (1982) *Information filing and finding.* ELM Publications.

BRITISH STANDARDS INSTITUTION (1969) *Alphabetical arrangement and the filing order of numerals and symbols.* B.S.I. (BS 1749).

BRITISH STANDARDS INSTITUTION (1970) *Page sizes for books.* B.S.I. (BS 1413).

BRITISH STANDARDS INSTITUTION (1970) *Abbreviation of titles of periodicals.* B.S.I. (BS 4148 Part 1).

BRITISH STANDARDS INSTITUTION (1976) *Recommendations for bibliographical references.* B.S.I. (BS 1629).

BRITISH STANDARDS INSTITUTION (1976) *Recommendations for the preparation of indexes to books, periodicals and other publications.* B.S.I. (BS 3700).

BRITISH STANDARDS INSTITUTION (1976) *Marks for copy preparation and proof correction.* B.S.I. (BS 5261C).

BRITISH STANDARDS INSTITUTION (1978) *Recommendations for citing publications by bibliographical references.* B.S.I. (BS 5605).

BUTCHER, Judith (1981) *Copy-editing: the Cambridge handbook.* 2nd ed. Cambridge University Press.

CAREY, G. V. (1971) *Mind the stop: a brief guide to punctuation, with a note on proof-correction.* Penguin.

COOPER, Bruce M. (1964) *Writing technical reports.* Penguin.

CRABB, George (1916, reprinted with corrections 1981) *Crabb's English synonyms.* Routledge.

CUTTS, Martin and MAHER, Chrissie (1980) *Writing plain English: why it should be done, how it's been done, how you can do it.* Whaley Bridge: Plain English Campaign.

FLETCHER, John (1983) *How to write a report.* Institute of Personnel Management.

FOWLER (1965) *Fowler's modern English usage.* 2nd ed. revised by Sir Ernest Gowers. Clarendon Press. (Paperback ed. 1983).

GILCHRIST, A. (1982) *System design and planning. In:* Handbook of special librarianship and information work. 5th ed. Editor: L. J. Anthony. Aslib. (Ch. 2).

GOWERS, Sir Ernest (1973) *The complete plain words.* 2nd ed. Revised by Sir Bruce Fraser. Penguin.

HART (1983) *Hart's rules for compositors and readers at the University Press Oxford.* 39th ed. Oxford University Press.

JAMES, David (1983) *Letter-writing.* Hodder and Stoughton.

KNIGHT, G. Norman (1979) *Indexing, the art of; a guide to the indexing of books and periodicals.* Allen & Unwin.

LIBRARY ASSOCIATION (1984) *Registration of Associates of the Library Association: regulations.* (Ref. ELR).

MILLER, Casey and SWIFT, Kate (1981) *Handbook of non-sexist writing for writers, editors and speakers.* Women's Press.

MITCHELL, John (1974) *How to write reports.* Fontana.

MOORE, Nick (1983) *How to do research.* Library Association.

NALGO (1983) *Watch your language! Non-sexist language: a guide for NALGO members.* NALGO.

NICHOLAS, R.M. and STANDLEY, A.E. (1984) *Basic bibliography book; a brief guide to compiling bibliographies.* ELM Publications.

NUTTALL (1979) *Nuttall dictionary of English synonyms and antonyms.* Edited by G. Elgie Christ. Warne.

OXFORD GUIDE (1983) *Oxford guide to English usage.* Compiled by E.S.C. Weiner. Clarendon Press.

PARTRIDGE, Eric (1963, revised reprint 1973) *Usage and abusage: a guide to good English..* Penguin.

PETERS, M.A. (1980) *The club treasurer's handbook: an essential guide to club accounting and administration.* Bristol: Rose-Jordan.

QUINN, Hestia (1982) *The club secretary's guide.* David & Charles.

RITCHIE, Sheila (editor) (1982) *Modern library practice.* 2nd ed. ELM Publications.

ROGET (1982) *Roget's thesaurus.* New edition prepared by Susan M. Lloyd. Longman. (Other editions published by Penguin and by Sphere).

SAVILLE, Tim and SAVILLE, Jenny (1981) *Business letter writer.* Ward Lock.

SCARLES, Christopher (1980) *Copyright.* Cambridge University Press.

SMITH, Keith (1980) *Marketing for small publishers.* Inter-Action Imprint.

SOCIETY OF INDEXERS (1984) *Indexers available 1984–85.* Society of Indexers.

TREWEEK, Chris and ZEITLYN, Jonathan (1983) *The alternative printing handbook.* Penguin.

TURK, Christopher and KIRKMAN, John (1982) *Effective writing: improving scientific, technical and business communication.* Spon.

WARD, Audrey and WARD, Philip (1979) *The small publisher: a manual and case histories.* Cambridge: Oleander Press.

WARD, R.A. (1977) *100% report writing: a guide for graduates and students.* Virginia Water: R. and H. Ward.

WOOD, Frederick T. (1981) *Current English usage.* Revised by R.H. Flavell and L.M. Flavell. Macmillan.

Writers' and artists' yearbook (1984) Black.

FURTHER READING

These publications, although not specifically cited in the preceding text, also provide useful information in relation to report writing and connected topics; those marked 'out of print' may be available in libraries and second hand from bookshops.

ALEXANDER, Louis (1984) *Word processing: a beginner's guide for authors. In:* Writers' and artists' yearbook. Black (p.457–464).

ALVAREZ, Joseph A. (1980) *The elements of technical writing.* New York: Harcourt, Brace, Jovanovich.

BENTLEY, Trevor J. (1978) *Report writing in business.* Institute of Cost and Management Accountants.

CRIX, Frederick C. (1979) *Reprographic management handbook.* 2nd ed. Business Books.

CURRAN, Susan (1984) *Word processing for beginners.* Granada.

DARBYSHIRE, A. E. (1970) *Report writing: the form and style of efficient communication.* Arnold. Out of print.

FLETCHER, J. A. and GOWING, D. F. (1980) *Effective writing for accountants.* Institute of Chartered Accountants in England and Wales.

INMAN, K. and SWINBURNE, J. (1972) *Introduction to flow charting.* Stockport: Polytech Publishers.

IRONMAN, Ralph (1966) *Writing the executive report: a guide to report writing for those engaged in science, technology and management.* Heinemann. Out of print.

McARTHUR, Tom (1981) *Longman lexicon of contemporary English,* Longman.

MARTYN, John and LANCASTER, F. Wilfrid (1981) *Investigative methods in library and information science : an introduction.* Arlington, Va.: Information Resources Press.

MEADOWS, Jack (1982) *Authors, publishers and word processors. In:* Multi-media communications. Edited by May Katzen. Frances Pinter. (Ch. 4).

NEW, Peter G. (1975) *Reprography for librarians.* Bingley.

ORNA, Liz (1983) *Writing to inform.* Chislehurst: Ravensbourne College of Art and Design.

INDEX

The index contains references to significant topics treated in Chapters 1 to 7 and to names found in those chapters and in the References and Further Reading sections.

Where there are several page references for an index term, major references are printed in **bold** type.

Pages giving illustrations are indicated by (ill.) and those providing bibliographical information by (bibl.).

Names of publications are printed in *italic*.

The alphabetical order is letter-by-letter (spaces and punctuation signs between words being ignored in filing).

PFB

Abbreviations
    in bibliographical references 17
    in glossaries 17
    in indexes 20
Abstracts (summaries) 7, **19**
Accommodation surveys 42
Acknowledgements . . . . . . 11, **18−19**
Acronyms 17, 25
Alexander, Louis . . . . 49 (bibl.)
Alphabetical order 21
Alvarez, Joseph A . . . . 49 (bibl.)
Anderson, M D . . . . 20, 46 (bibl.)
Annual reports
    (*see also* Financial reports; Progress reports) 38
Anthony, L J . . . . 46 (bibl.), 47 (bibl.)
Appendixes 16, **18**, 30
Ashe, Geoffrey . . . . 25, 46 (bibl.)
Asterisks for footnotes 11

Balance sheets 41
Bentley, Trevor J . . . . 49 (bibl.)
Bibliographical references . . 11, **17−18**
Binding
    (*see also* Covers) . . . . . . **32−33**, 35
Blagden, J . . . . 41, 46 (bibl.)
Bold type for emphasis 30
Booth, Pat F . . . . 20, 46 (bibl.)
Briefing documents 2
British Standards Institution (BSI)
     . . . . .17, 18, 20, 21, 29, 31, 46 (bibl.)
Budget reports . . . . 41−42
Bulletins 1
Butcher, Judith
     . . 11, 18, 20, 26, 29, 30, 31, 46 (bibl.)

Capital letters
    for highlighting 30
    in words and phrases 26
Captions (titles)
    appendixes 18
    illustrations 16
Carbon copies 30, 32
Carey, G V . . . . 26, 46 (bibl.)
Charts . . . . 12 (ill.), 16
Christ, G Elgie . . . . 47 (bibl.)
Chronologies 10
Citations (bibliographical references)
     . . . . 11, **17−18**
Communication . . . . 1, 3−4
Computers, filing rules 21
Confidentiality, personnel reports . . 40
Content . . . . 10−22
Contents lists 22
Cooper, Bruce M . . . . 12, 25, 46 (bibl.)
Copy preparation . . . . 28−33
Copyright
    information on title page 21
    of quotations . . . . . . 11, 18−19
Covers
    (*see also* Binding) 21, 32
Crabb, George . . . . 24, 46 (bibl.)
Crix, Frederick C . . . . 49 (bibl.)
Curran, Susan . . . . 49 (bibl.)
Cutts, Martin . . . . 25, 47 (bibl.)

'Daggers' for footnotes 11
Darbyshire, A E . . . . 49 (bibl.)
Date on title page 21
Departmental reports
    (*see also* Annual reports; Personnel reports) 36

Diagrams
  see Illustrations
Distribution 7, 43–44
Document (*definition*) 1

English language. 23–26
Evaluation (system) reports 38–40

Fault-finding reports 38–40
Feedback from reports 45
Filing order 21
Financial reports 41–42
Flavell, L M . . . . 48 (bibl.)
Flavell, R H . . . . 48 (bibl.)
Fletcher, John. . . . . 12, 47 (bibl.)
Fletcher, J A. . . . . 49 (bibl.)
Flowcharts. 12, 16, 39
'Fog Index' 25
Footnotes 11, 24, 41
Foreign words. 26
Foreword 19
Fowler's modern English usage
. . . . 23, 47 (bibl.)
Fraser, Bruce . . . . 47 (bibl.)

Gilchrist, A . . . . 12, 47 (bibl.)
Glossaries 17, 24
Gowers, Ernest . . . . 23, 47 (bibl.)
Gowing, D F. . . . . 49 (bibl.)
Grammar. 26
Graphs . . . . 13 (ill.), 16
Gunning, R 25

Half-tones
  (*see also* Photographs) 16
Handwritten copies 28, 30
Hart's rules. . . . . .26, 30, 47 (bibl.)
Headings 9–10, 22, 38
House style
  bibliographical references . . .17–18
  spelling. 26
Humour 6, 27

Illustrations 10, 11–17, 39
  layout 30
  lists 21
Income and expenditure accounts . . 41
Indexes. 20–21, 31
  layout 30
Inman, K. . . . . 49 (bibl.)
Ironman, Ralph . . . . 49 (bibl.)

Irony 27
ISBN (International Standard Book
  Number 21
Italic type for emphasis 30

James, David. . . . . .44, 47 (bibl.)
Jargon 24

Katzen, May. . . . . 49 (bibl.)
Kirkman, John . . 12, 25, 44, 48 (bibl.)
Knight, G Norman, ... 20, 47 (bibl.)

LA (Library Association) . 35, 47 (bibl.)
Lancaster, F Wilfrid . . . . . . 49 (bibl.)
Language. 23–26, 39
Layout. 29–30
Length of report 29
Letter-by-letter alphabetical order . . 21
Lettering
  in captions. 16
  variation, for highlighting 30
Letters accompanying reports 44
Library Association. . . . . 35, 47 (bibl.)
Lloyd, Susan M . . . . 48 (bibl.)

McArthur, Tom . . . . 49 (bibl.)
Maher, Chrissie . . . . 25, 47 (bibl.)
Martyn, John . . . . 49 (bibl.)
Master copies 30–31
Meadows, Jack . . . . 49 (bibl.)
Meetings reports. 37–38
Memoranda 2
Messages 5–7
Microfiches for illustrations, supplementary data 17, 32
Miller, Casey . . . . 24, 47 (bibl.)
Minutes of meetings 1, 37–38
Mitchell, John . . . . 12, 47 (bibl.)
Moore, Nick . . . . . . .11, 37, 47 (bibl.)

NALGO . . . . 24, 47 (bibl.)
New, Peter G . . . . 49 (bibl.)
Nicholas, R M . . . . 18, 47 (bibl.)
Numbering.
  appendixes. 18
  bibliographical references 18
  footnotes. 11
  pages 22
  sections. 9–10
Nuttall dictionary . . . . . . 24, 47 (bibl.)

51

Oral communication 2–3
Oral presentation or reports 44–45
Orna, Liz. . . . . 49 (bibl.)
Oxford guide . . . . 23, 47 (bibl.)

Page numbers, contents lists 22
Pages, number and size 29
Paper
    sizes. 29
    types 32
Paragraph numbering 9–10
Partridge, Eric . . . . 24, 48 (bibl.)
Performance appraisal reports . . . 40–41
Personal development reports . . . 35–36
Personnel reports 40–41
Peters, M.A . . . . 41, 48 (bibl.)
Photocopying 32
Photographs 16, 39
Pie charts. . . . . 12 (ill.)
Plain English. 25–26
Preface 19
Printers name on title page. 21
Printing. 30, 32
Professional development reports
    . . . . **35–36**, 44
Progress reports
    departmental 36
    personal 35–36, 40–41
Proof correction. 31
Punctuation 26
Purpose. 5

Questionnaires. 34, 42
Quinn, Hestia . . . . 38, 48 (bibl.)
Quotations. 11

Racist language 24
Readability formula 25
Readers, recipients 7, 24
References, bibliographical . 11, **17–18**
Repetition 26
Report (*definition*) 1–2
Reproduction 28, 30–32
Research reports
  (*see also* Student project reports). 37
Ritchie, Sheila. . . . . 40, 48 (bibl.)
Roget's thesaurus . . . . . . 24, 48 (bibl.)

Saville, Jenny . . . . 44, 48 (bibl.)
Saville, Tim . . . . 44, 48 (bibl.)
Scarles, Christopher. . . . . 11, 48 (bibl.)
Self-presentation 35–36
Self-publishing. 32
Series name on title page. 21
Sexist language 24
Sizes of paper 29
Smith, Keith. 32

Society of Indexers . . . . . 20, 48 (bibl.)
South, M L. . . . . 20, 46 (bibl.)
Special language. **24–25**, 39
Spelling. 26
Spoken (oral) communication. . . . 2–3
Sponsors' names on title page
  (*see also* Acknowledgements) . . . 21
Standard Book Numbering Agency . . 21
Standley, A E . . . . 18, 47 (bibl.)
Structure
  (*see also* particular types of report,
  e.g. Financial reports) . . . **8–10**, 29
Student project reports
  (*see also* Research reports) **34–35**, 44
Style 23–27
Subjects (topics) **5–6**, 34
Summaries (abstracts) 7, **19**
Superscript numbers
    footnotes. 11
    references 18
Swift, Kate. . . . . 24, 47 (bibl.)
Swinburne, J. . . . . 49 (bibl.)
System evaluation reports 38–40

Tables 12–16
Technical language **24–25**, 39
Title pages 21, 31
Titles
  (*see also* Caption: Headings). **5–6**, 31
Tone 23, **26–27**
Topics **5–6**, 34
Treweek, Chris . . . . 32, 48 (bibl.)
Turk, Christopher, 12, 25, 44, 48 (bibl.)
Typographical variation 30
    in indexes 20

Vocabulary
  (*see also* Glossaries). 24–26

Ward, Audrey . . . . 32, 48 (bibl.)
Ward, Philip . . . . 32, 48 (bibl.)
Ward, R A . . . . 12, 48 (bibl.)
Weiner, E S C . . . . 47 (bibl.)
Wood, Frederick T . . . . . 24, 48 (bibl.)
Word-by-word alphabetical order . . . 21
Word processors
    filing rules 21
    typographical variation. 30
Words, number of. 29, 35
Writers' and artists' yearbook
  . . . . . 11, 21, 31, 48 (bibl.), 49 (bibl.)
Written communication 2–3

Zeitlyn, Jonathan . . . . . . 32, 48 (bibl.)

OTHER BOOKS FROM ELM PUBLICATIONS

Modern library practice: a manual & textbook
edited by Sheila Ritchie
A5 £8.90 352 pp. Index isbn 0 9506828 5 9

Modern library practice: tutor's pack Advanced (B)
by Mike Perry et al
A4 binder £15.95 non-net isbn 0 9505828 7 5

Modern library practice: tutor's pack Basic (A)
by Sheila Ritchie and Sonia Sayed
A4 binder £11.95 non-net isbn 0 9505828 6 7

Information filing & finding: a basic guide
by Pat F Booth & M L South
A5 sewn pbk £7.90 320pp. Index isbn 0 946139 08

Personnel management in context, the 1980s
by Terry McIlwee
A5 sewn pbk £7.90 352 pp. isbn 0 9505828 8 3

Personnel management in context
manpower statistics supplement
Tables and data to accompany the textbook
A4 looseleaf £2.90 non-net isbn 0 9505828 9 1

People in organisations
second edition
by Pat Armstrong & Chris Dawson
A5 hdbk £9.90 isbn 0 946139 10 5
A5 pbk £6.90 isbn 0 946139 25 3